My essay details

Name:

Year:

Subject:

Teacher:

Due date:

Word or page limit:

Essay Question:

First published by Brio Books in 2020
Reprinted in 2022

ISBN 9781922267368

Published in Australia and New Zealand by:

Brio Books, an imprint of Booktopia Group Ltd
Unit E1, 3-29 Birnie Avenue, Lidcombe, NSW 2141, Australia
briobooks.com.au

Printed and bound in Australia by Pegasus Media & Logistics

MIX
Paper from responsible sources
FSC® C008194
FSC www.fsc.org

The paper in this book is FSC® certified. FSC® promotes environmentally responsible, socially beneficial and economically viable management of the world's forests.

So, you have an essay to write. Don't panic.
Don't over-think it. Don't put it off any longer.
Simply turn the page and get to work.

Plan

First things first

Where and when you learn best

Writing an essay is not just about knowing what to write, it is also about knowing your own strengths, limitations, what conditions you need to concentrate well and write your best. Think about where and when you learn best to complete the graphic organiser on the following page.

Time you normally fall asleep	Time you feel most unproductive	Best time for you to study

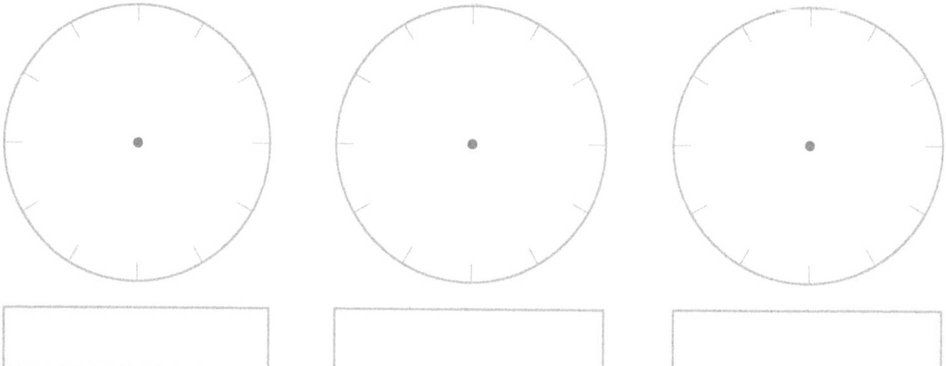

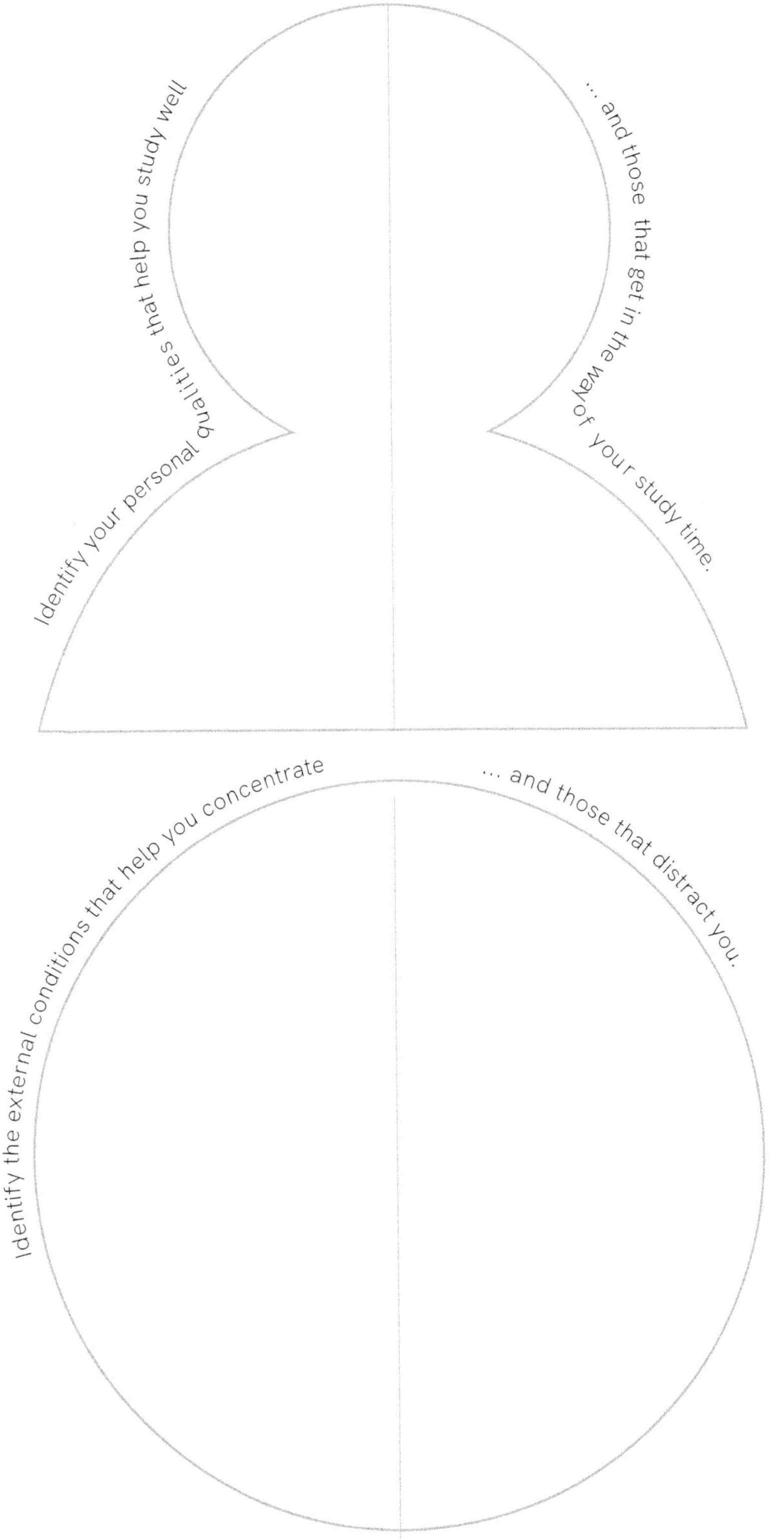
Identify your personal qualities that help you study well
... and those that get in the way of your study time.
Identify the external conditions that help you concentrate
... and those that distract you.

How will you use your time?

When is your essay due? Write the due date on the bottom line of the table, and then work backwards to today. How much time do you have? Do you have other essays or exams that you also need to find time to study for? Allocate time for editing closest to the due date, then writing and researching – keeping all your obligations in mind. You can start planning your essay from today.

MONDAY	TUESDAY	WEDNESDAY	THURSDAY	FRIDAY	SATURDAY	SUNDAY

Date due: ____________________

The essay question

The first step in writing a good essay is to understand what the question is really asking. Even though you wrote the question on the front page, write it out again here. This time, also say it aloud to yourself as you write (writing and hearing your question multiple times helps you begin to better understand its meaning).

What is your question asking you to do?

Your question is not only asking you about a topic, it is prompting you to do something with that topic. For this reason, your teacher might refer to your essay question as an essay prompt (or an essay stimulus, topic or statement). Whether it is phrased as a question or a prompt, look for the verb which will ask you to argue, define, explore, review, explain, compare or contrast aspects of the topic. In the space below, write the verb and its meaning (look up the meaning of the verb in a dictionary or use an online glossary) so you understand exactly what you are being asked to do.

Verb	Meaning

GET THIS! It can be useful to think about verbs in a real-world setting. For example, if your essay asks you to *explore* a topic, ask yourself: 'What does an explorer do?' Your answer might be that an explorer sets out to find new things, to follow paths that look interesting, to pay attention to small details and discover new places. So, in an essay, when you are asked to explore your topic, you are being asked to search the detail of your topic for new or different ways of thinking about it, to look for more information than your teacher gives you, to question why things are the way they are, and to discover new insights about the text.

HELP! What if there is no verb? Occasionally, essay questions are written as prompts (stimulus, topics, statements) without a verb — they are verbless. If you get given a verbless essay question, you can uncover the implied verb by asking yourself: 'What is this question asking me to do?'

WHAT IF THERE IS MORE THAN ONE VERB? Occasionally, essay questions are written with two or more verbs. Analyse the question to decide whether one verb is central to answering the question or if each matters equally. Either way, define the meaning of all verbs in your question with a dictionary or online glossary.

WHO CARES? You could write the best essay in the world, but if you ignore the verb, or misunderstand its meaning, your essay response will not properly address the question and you will not get the mark you could have. An essay question is not only asking you about a topic, it is asking you *to do* something specific with information on that topic.

What is the main topic or concept in your question?

Your question will ask you to write about a particular topic or concept. Usually, it will be a topic or concept that you have covered in class. Identify the topic or concept in your question and briefly define it in your own words.

HELP! Sometimes your question will be focused on one topic or concept, but also include sub-questions. Ask yourself: Are there multiple aspects to your question? Are some aspects of your question more important than others? Can you see any sub-questions? Check with your teacher if you're unsure.

What about the marking criteria?

Write out the marking criteria if your teacher has listed it. Much like the verb in the question, the marking criteria is another tool that you can use to help guide your response to the question. Can you see how the marking criteria can potentially guide your response to the question? What is the marking criteria encouraging you to focus on?

Uncover what you think the question is asking in point form

After considering the verb, the main topic and the marking criteria, use your own words to dot point what your essay question is asking you to do.

Talk to a friend

Explain your understanding of the question to a friend. If they are writing an essay on the same essay question, compare your notes. Do you have the same understanding of what you are being asked to do? Is there anything you need to check with your teacher? Write your questions below.

Start thinking

Now that you have pulled the question apart and understand what it's asking, it's time to start thinking about your own response.

Storming your brain

Set a stopwatch for two minutes and write down everything you can think of on your essay topic in that time, even if your ideas seem irrelevant or nonsensical. One of the best ways to train yourself to be effective at brainstorming is to begin writing your ideas down without stopping, censoring, or judging them. Keep writing point after point. Let it flow. Let your mind focus on the next thought that pops into your head and write it down, even if it has nothing to do with your essay.

Although some of what you brainstorm will be useless, you will also find a great deal of useful information swimming about in your brain. Get your ideas out: think freely, draw pictures and diagrams or mind maps, write in point form, write single words or talk out loud.

GET THIS! As a noun, the word 'storming' means 'the sudden forceful attack and capture of a building or other place by troops'. So brainstorming is capturing your brain with the sudden and energetic attack of as many ideas as you can think of. As an adjective, 'storming' is also used to describe a performance that is 'outstandingly vigorous or impressive'. The power of the brainstorm, then, is in the speed and energy you generate to think of many ideas as possible. Make yours outstandingly vigorous and impressive!

BRAINSTORM YOUR IDEAS HERE

Putting your ideas into groups

In this section, you can organise the random thoughts from your brainstorm into groups of related ideas. Arranging your ideas in this way allows you to make sense of your brainstorm and to consider your ideas in terms of their relationships to one another as well as to the big picture of your essay.

Give each group of ideas a title that summarises the content of the ideas. You will get more ideas once you begin researching, so don't worry if you only have a few groups right now. That's all you need to begin.

WHO CARES? Your essay question only exists to prompt or stimulate your thinking. The thing that matters is what you decide to do with the topic of the essay question – the way you take the question and craft your response. Brainstorming and grouping your ideas are the start of understanding the question, but also the start of creating your own unique response.

GROUP 1	GROUP 2	GROUP 3

Figuring out your main point

Do you ever feel that you don't know what you're really trying to say in your essay? You might have the information and understand the topic, but still feel unsure what to do with it once you start writing. If this happens to you, your papers are lacking a direction, otherwise known as a main point. Every essay should communicate a main point to the reader. This is often called a thesis, or at this stage of the essay writing process, a predictive thesis. It is a predictive thesis because it is simply what you predict or forecast your main point will be: it is your best guess.

Figuring out the main point of your essay is a work in progress. Over time, it will develop from your best guess to a clear point that you have carefully considered. But for now, it's a guess. So, considering the ideas you generated in your brainstorm and the way you grouped them together – but also casting your mind back to the essay question, the verb, the topic of the question and the marking criteria – can you think what the main point of your essay might be? Don't panic if you're not sure yet or if you can't articulate it perfectly. You are at the very beginning of the writing process; just write down what you think your main point might be as a predictive thesis.

HELP! Not sure how to think of a predictive thesis? Try to answer these questions: What are your first impressions of your essay question? Do you like the topic? What do you like/not like about it? Do you agree or disagree with the question? Are there parts of the essay question that interest you more than others? Given your responses to these questions, can you say which direction your views are leaning? That direction is your predictive thesis.

Research

Start researching

Now that you have some good ideas for what you could include in your essay, you can start to think about what evidence you will use to defend your main point.

GET THIS! A person who writes essays is called an essayist — that makes you an essayist!

Summarising your main text

Your teacher may give you a graphic organiser worksheet to help you summarise the type of text relevant to your essay (your main text may be a novel, play, poetry, short story, newspaper, magazine article or film). Or, if your question asks you to consider particular characters in the text, your teacher may give you a worksheet to help you analyse characters. Paste any additional worksheets on the following page.

PASTE IN YOUR WORKSHEET HERE

PASTE IN YOUR WORKSHEET HERE

Taking notes from your texts

Taking notes while you read is not just writing down points of interest but is a way of processing the information you read to find the topics and specific evidence you will use in your essay. The note-taking worksheets on the following pages will help you consider the evidence in your texts that might be useful in the essay response you write.

You may also need to find additional texts or sources that provide more evidence to better defend the main point of your essay. You can use the note-taking worksheets on the following pages to record your ideas from any additional sources you read.

HELP! Thinking and reading critically are essential tools for essayists. Being critical in this context means that you question what you hear and read as you seek to understand a range of views on the topic. Ask yourself: Why has the author written in this way? What purpose does it have? Why has the author addressed certain topics and left out others? What does this tell me about this piece of writing? Are there gaps in the argument? How persuasive is the writing? Why? What evidence does the author use to convince me? How does the perspective presented in this text support or challenge my own thoughts on this topic?

Text details

Title:

Author:

Year published:

Publisher:

Text summary

This text is about:

Evidence

Three pieces of relevant information from this text are:

1.	2.	3.

Great quotes

Choose your favourite direct quotes. Make sure you write them inside 'quotation marks' and put the page number the quote is from in brackets at the end.

Note to self

After examining this text, what new ideas do you have for your own essay response?

Text details

Title:

Author:

Year published:

Publisher:

Text summary

This text is about:

Evidence

Three pieces of relevant information from this text are:

1.	2.	3.

Great quotes

Choose your favourite direct quotes. Make sure you write them inside 'quotation marks' and put the page number the quote is from in brackets at the end.

Note to self

After examining this text, what new ideas do you have for your own essay response?

Text details Title: Author: Year published: Publisher:
Text summary This text is about:
Evidence Three pieces of relevant information from this text are:

1.	2.	3.

Great quotes

Choose your favourite direct quotes. Make sure you write them inside 'quotation marks' and put the page number the quote is from in brackets at the end.

Note to self

After examining this text, what new ideas do you have for your own essay response?

Text details

Title:

Author:

Year published:

Publisher:

Text summary

This text is about:

Evidence

Three pieces of relevant information from this text are:

1.	2.	3.

Great quotes

Choose your favourite direct quotes. Make sure you write them inside 'quotation marks' and put the page number the quote is from in brackets at the end.

Note to self

After examining this text, what new ideas do you have for your own essay response?

Analysing ideas

Behind the scenes of your perfectly presented final essay will be a pile of messy notes and discarded ideas. Every essayist analyses many ideas before settling on the final main point (or thesis) of their essay. Your teacher has a range of graphic organiser worksheets that may help you analyse ideas and consider things like language structures, features and devices as well as the relationship of texts to their historical, social and cultural contexts. Ask your teacher for worksheets relevant to your essay question and paste them in on the following pages.

WHO CARES? The more deeply you analyse and think about various aspects of your essay topic now, the easier it will be to write your final draft. If you put great effort into planning and researching what you are going to write about, your essay will practically write itself! The graphic organiser worksheets your teacher gives you will help you to think deeply and analyse well.

PASTE IN YOUR WORKSHEET HERE

PASTE IN YOUR WORKSHEET HERE

PASTE IN YOUR WORKSHEET HERE

PASTE IN YOUR WORKSHEET HERE

Write

Before you start

It is tempting to start writing as soon as you feel you have something to say but first, take a moment to clarify your main point and create an essay outline. This process will not only help you to develop a tidy, logical structure, but it will also take away much of the stress you can feel when writing. Drafting an essay without a main point or an outline is like travelling in an unfamiliar place without a destination or a map: it is difficult, confusing, and you're likely to get lost and frustrated. However, with a clear understanding of your destination (your main point, or thesis) and a good map in hand (your well-defined outline), all you'll need to do when you sit down to write is relax and follow the path you have set for yourself. And, even though the path may change as you begin writing (often our ideas develop in the process of actually writing about a topic, not just thinking about it), your good planning and research will mean that you will be prepared and able to adapt to any changes you introduce without losing direction.

Clarify your main point

Now that you have conducted your research and taken notes on each of your texts, you can use your more developed ideas to revisit (or create, if you weren't able to do it earlier in your predictive thesis) the main point of your essay. Use the graphic organiser on the following page to help you decide on your main point, the topics you will address in each paragraph and what evidence you will draw on to support those topics and your main point.
Answer the following questions:

- What is the main point or thesis of your essay?
- What is your opinion or position on the main subject, topic or concept of your essay question? Do you agree or disagree with the question?
- What is your stance on the question?
- What topics will you include to explain your main point? Each topic you identify on the worksheet will become one paragraph of your essay (depending on the length or scope of your essay, you may need to add more topics)?
- What evidence do you need to support the topic of each paragraph?
- Does the information come from within your main text, or from an additional text or source?

HELP! What is referencing? If your teacher has asked you to reference in your essay, you will need to cite the sources you use as evidence. Ask your teacher for the graphic organiser worksheets on referencing and avoiding plagiarism.

CONCEPT MAP

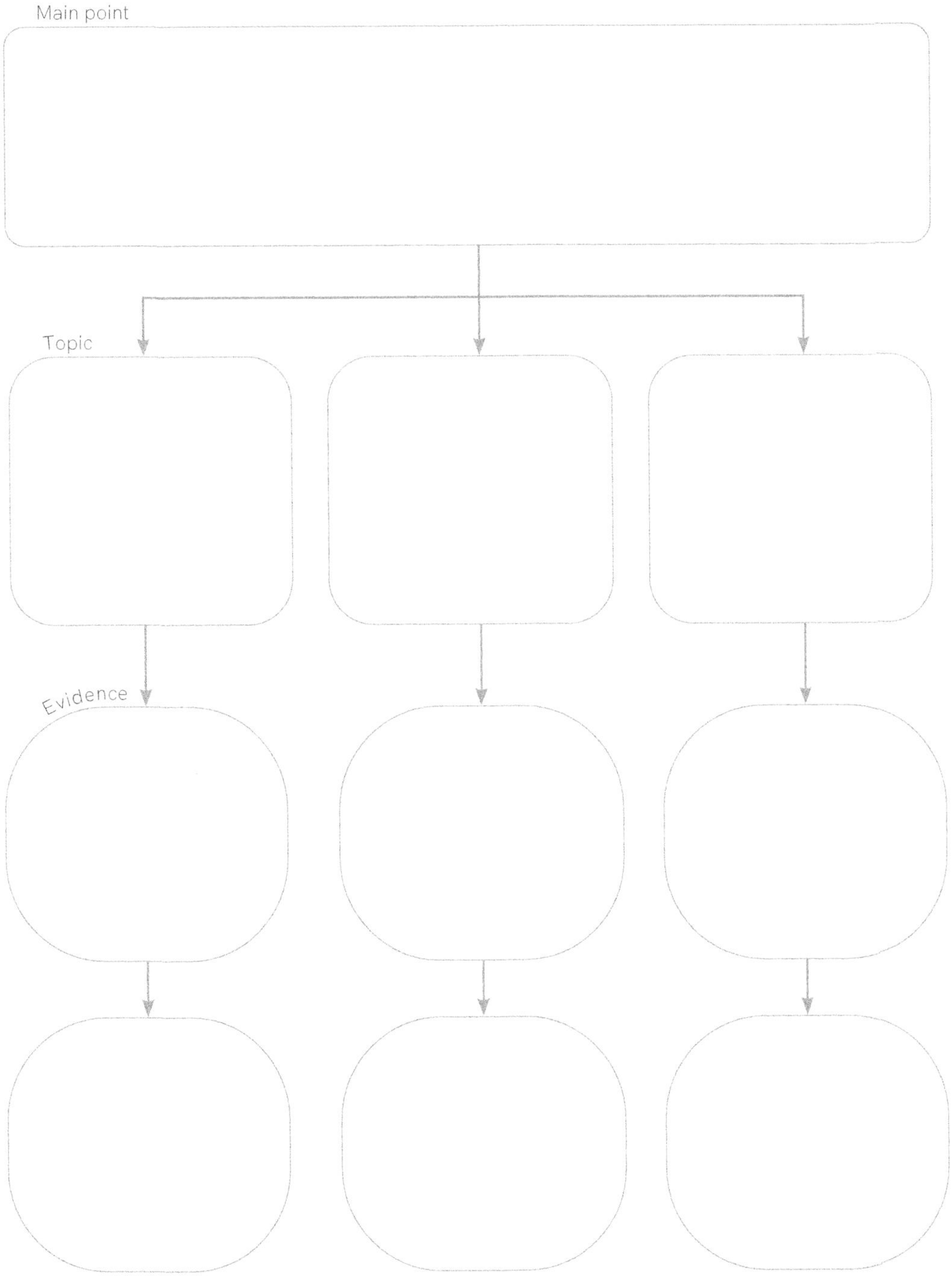

Now, create your thesis statement

You have identified your main point and you know what topics you are going to use in your essay to support your main point; now you need to create your thesis statement. Your thesis statement is one sentence that tells the reader what your main point is and why. It is, most simply, a statement of your thesis. Look back at the graphic organiser you just completed: you have clearly identified your main point (the what), and the paragraph topics you have already identified are the basic reasons you are defending your main point (they are the why). So, to write your thesis statement you need to bring your main point and your paragraph topics together in a complete sentence.

My thesis statement

____

(state your main point)

____

____________________________________ because

____

____ ,

(topic 1)

____

____ ,

(topic 2)

____

____ .

(topic 3)

Your thesis statement helps you to clearly and concisely state the core of your essay response. It should be written in the introduction and conclusion of your essay. The following section shows you how to do that.

Essay structure: create an outline

The basic structure of a well-organised essay has a certain shape and flow that can be shown in a flow chart such as the one on the next page. This is a simple illustration that outlines how to logically and coherently structure your essay from the introduction to the body and the conclusion. You can visualise the big picture of your essay structure and argument using this diagram and then organise your own essay in the same way. Many students have good things to say in their essays, but they don't present the information in a clear or logical way. If you want to get good marks, you must spend some time developing a logical structure to your essay. Ask yourself: in what order will I present my information so it makes the most sense and builds the strongest and clearest argument? How can I organise my topics to lead naturally and logically from one idea to the next? Once your outline is complete, you will be ready to start writing.

GET THIS! Creating an outline of your essay will give you a clear starting point. Once you start writing, you may find that your plan requires a little adjusting, so don't be too fussy about getting this plan perfect now. While it is important to be comprehensive, your outline is just a guide, a plan of attack to develop the structure of your essay, and you can change it as you go.

Introduction	1. **Opening sentence:** start with a general statement on the essay question 2. **Introduce each topic** in the order you will cover them in your essay 3. **State your main point** towards the end of your introduction in the form of a thesis statement.

First body paragraph	1. **Topic sentence:** state the topic of this paragraph 2. **Present information and evidence** to support your assertions 3. **Linking sentence:** end your paragraph with a sentence that connects it to the next paragraph

Second body paragraph	1. **Topic sentence:** state the topic of this paragraph 2. **Present information and evidence** to support your assertions 3. **Linking sentence:** end your paragraph with a sentence that connects it to the next paragraph

Third body paragraph	1. **Topic sentence:** state the topic of this paragraph 2. **Present information and evidence** to support your assertions 3. **Linking sentence:** end your paragraph with a sentence that connects it to the next paragraph

Conclusion	1. **Restate your main point** in the form of a thesis statement. 2. **Summarise and review the topics** you covered in the body of your essay—this is our last chance to remind the reader why the information you have given is important! 3. **Do not introduce new ideas**

Constructing the introduction

The purpose of an introduction is to launch your main point. Here, the reader gets to hear what you are going to say for the first time. Opening with a general statement on the topic is a good strategy. The first sentence can interest the reader, or lose them completely. Some writers like to use a catchy quote, a statistic, or an anecdote (a brief, funny story) that introduces the topic.

You also need to present the sequence of topics that you will raise in the body of the paper (in the same order in which you will cover them in the body of your essay) and clearly present the main point of your essay in the form of a thesis statement.

OPENING SENTENCE:

INTRODUCE EACH TOPIC YOU WILL COVER IN ORDER:

STATE YOUR MAIN POINT IN THE FORM OF A THESIS STATEMENT:

Constructing the body

The body of your essay consists of everything between the introduction and conclusion. Here, you develop and build your argument by using the supporting information you have gathered during your research and summarised on your concept map on page 37. Generally, each paragraph in the body of your essay will look at a specific topic so you can think of each topic and its supporting information as one paragraph in the body of your essay. The questions to ask are: in which order will you present the information from your concept map? Which topic should go first, second and third? Within each paragraph topic, which piece of information will you present first, second, etc. Keep the main point of your essay in mind as you develop the body of your essay. Review your outline once you have planned it out. Does it make good, logical sense? Do you need to move anything around?

HELP! What are topic and linking sentences? A topic sentence is usually the first sentence in a paragraph and its job is to clearly introduce the topic of the paragraph. A linking sentence (sometimes called a transition sentence) is usually the last sentence in a paragraph and its job is to help the reader move (or transition) from one topic to the next, making the connection (or link) between them explicit. Your essay should read as one continuous, cohesive argument. It is the quality of your linking sentences that will help you to achieve that goal.

TOPIC SENTENCE:

EVIDENCE:

LINKING SENTENCE:

TOPIC SENTENCE:

EVIDENCE:

LINKING SENTENCE:

TOPIC SENTENCE:

EVIDENCE:

LINKING SENTENCE:

HOW DOES EACH PARAGRAPH DEFEND YOUR MAIN POINT?

Constructing the conclusion

The purpose of a conclusion is to repeat your major points, to tie your essay's argument together and to leave the reader with a strong idea of your essay's purpose. The conclusion should be a mirror image of your introduction. Here, you begin by clearly restating your main point. Then, revise the topics you wrote about in the body of your essay and end with a general, conclusive statement on the broad topic of your essay. Don't be tempted to introduce any new topics or ideas in your conclusion. The conclusion should bring your essay to an end, not give the reader new topics to think about or leave them with unanswered questions.

RESTATE YOUR MAIN POINT IN THE FORM OF A THESIS STATEMENT:

SUMMARISE YOUR MAIN TOPICS:

GENERAL CONCLUDING STATEMENT:

First draft

Congratulations, you are now ready to start writing! Using your essay outline as a guide, type your essay. You can print a copy and glue it in the following pages. Or, if you are practising handwriting, you can write your essay here.

GET THIS! There is no right or wrong way to start writing an essay. Some people leave the introduction to write last and begin by writing the body or even the conclusion. However, if you write your introduction first and then revise parts of your argument as you write, you will need to go back and make sure your introduction still reflects what is written in your final essay. Changing one part of your essay may affect the meaning of other sections. If you rewrite or change any part of your essay, make sure you think about its impact on the essay as a whole and adjust your introduction and conclusion to fit.

Final checks

Quick structure checklist

Use this checklist to give the structure of your essay a quick once-over:

INTRODUCTION

Have you:

- ☐ started with a catchy sentence, interesting quote, or relevant anecdote?
- ☐ introduced the topic of the essay and any major terms?
- ☐ presented each topic, in the order you will cover them, in the body of the essay?
- ☐ ended with a strong, clear statement on your main point in the form of a thesis statement?

BODY

Have you:

- ☐ used topic sentences in each paragraph?
- ☐ written clear, to-the-point paragraphs?
- ☐ kept a logical flow and constructed a logical argument?
- ☐ regularly drawn links to your main point?
- ☐ referenced the evidence you cite from other texts and sources if your teacher asked you to reference in your essay?
- ☐ connected paragraphs together with linking sentences?

CONCLUSION

Have you:

- ☐ summarised your main point by restating your thesis statement?
- ☐ restated how your evidence supports your main point?
- ☐ made sure not to introduce any new ideas?
- ☐ ended with a general concluding statement?
- ☐ stayed within the word limit?
- ☐ included a Reference List or Bibliography if your teacher asked you to reference in your essay?

HELP! You've written too many words. Your essay is due tomorrow. You don't know what to cut out. In general, your introduction should be 15% of the word limit, the conclusion should be 10% of the word limit, and the body should be 75% of the word limit. So, for a 1000-word essay, your introduction should be 150 words, your conclusion should be 100 words and the body of your essay should be 750 words. If your essay is too long, check the word limit of your essay and work out how long each section should be. Then, cut where necessary. Sticking to these percentages (15%-75%-10%) will help to structure and balance your essay.

Editing your own essay

Editing involves proofreading for spelling and grammatical errors as well as making sure the structure works. You need to correct any mistakes in your essay and check that you have clearly and logically said what you think you have. Re-read your essay aloud as this will help you notice errors. Words, sentences and phrases that look fine when written may sound very different when you hear them spoken.

Ask yourself the following questions and put a tick next to each one when you're done:

☐ Is my main point clear?

Have you stated your thesis clearly in your introduction and restated it in your conclusion?

☐ Is my argument clearly developed?

Your argument will be clearly developed if you can see how each paragraph is convincing the reader of your main point.

☐ Does my essay flow?

Do you have topic and linking sentences in each paragraph?

☐ Have I been too wordy?

If any part of your essay sounds long-winded or unclear, step back and ask yourself: 'In simple terms, what am I trying to say here?' Then change what you have written to the clear, direct version in plain English. It may not be a literary masterpiece, but it will get your message across, and in academic essay writing, that is your main aim.

☐ Have I made spelling, grammar or punctuation mistakes?

Spelling does not come naturally for many of us. And although it is not a measure of intelligence, most teachers will tell you how annoying it is to receive papers full of spelling mistakes. Some teachers may even take marks away for too many spelling errors. It does seem cruel to be marked on little things like spelling, but often it is the fine details that make the difference between a good mark and a top mark. Imagine, in all the reading you have had to do for this essay, that you constantly had to battle through typos, spelling mistakes, and poor grammar in other people's writing. It would get pretty frustrating and annoying. Accurate spelling, use of grammar and punctuation matter because they instruct the reader how to read your writing. You don't have to be a good speller or understand every grammatical and punctuation rule in the English language, but you do need to check for obvious mistakes.

☐ Have I included a Bibliography or Reference List?

(This is only if your teacher asked you to reference)

☐ Do I need to ask for help?

If you are having trouble with proofreading your essay, ask your teacher or librarian for help. You can also swap essays with a friend and check each other's work. Use the Editor's Checklist on the next page.

Editing a friend's essay

Swap your essay with a friend and be each other's editor. Use the Editor's Checklist below to give each other feedback.

✔	**Editor's Checklist**
	Clearly stated main point
	Clearly developed argument
	Clearly structured introduction
	Clearly structured body
	Clearly structured conclusion
	Clearly written paragraphs each addressing one topic
	Clearly stated topic and linking sentences in each paragraph
	Simple, direct language
	Perfect spelling
	Perfect grammar

The things I noticed you did well are ...	
One thing I noticed you could change that might improve your mark is ...	

Feedback

When you receive your mark for your essay, your teacher should give you some comments on what you did well and where your essay could have been improved. If you don't get any comments, ask your teacher for feedback. Then, consider your teacher's notes and reflect on what you have learnt.

WHO CARES? It is important to know what you did well (so you can do it again next time) and what you didn't do well (so you can learn from it and avoid the same mistake in the future). Getting constructive feedback on your writing is one of the best ways to improve your skills.

Feedback from your teacher:

Reflecting on your teacher's feedback, dot point what you have learnt:

Congratulations!

You nailed your essay!